# Shit
# I Can't
# Remember

# hello!

this password organizer is
very important to me, so...

**IF FOUND**

*Please*
RETURN TO

_____

_____

# hello!

this password organizer is
very important to me, so...

IF FOUND

Please
RETURN TO

_____

_____

# PASSWORD
*keeper*

NAME :

_____

PHONE :

_____

EMAIL ADDRESS :

_____

ADDRESS :



_____

EMERGENCY CONTACTS :

# Birthday Dates to Remember!

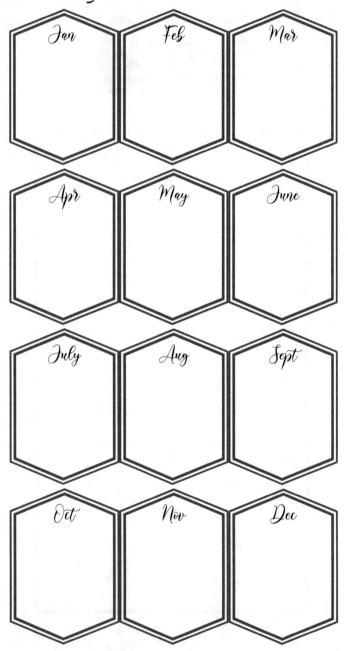

Jan

Feb

Mar

Apr

May

June

July

Aug

Sept

Oct

Nov

Dec

# social media password tracker

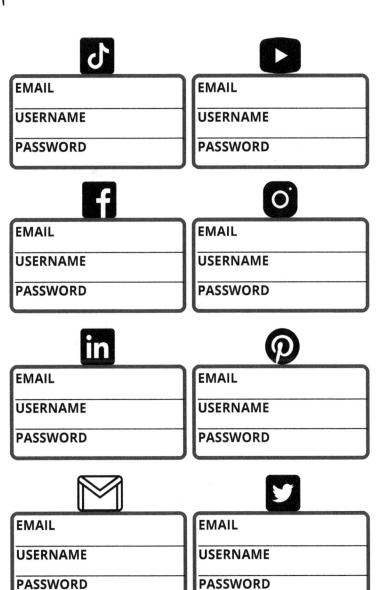

**EMAIL**

**USERNAME**

**PASSWORD**

**EMAIL**

**USERNAME**

**PASSWORD**

**EMAIL**

**USERNAME**

**PASSWORD**

**EMAIL**

**USERNAME**

**PASSWORD**

**EMAIL**

**USERNAME**

**PASSWORD**

**EMAIL**

**USERNAME**

**PASSWORD**

**EMAIL**

**USERNAME**

**PASSWORD**

**EMAIL**

**USERNAME**

**PASSWORD**

# WTF IS MY PASSWORD?

**WEBSITE**

**USERNAME**

**PASSWORD**

**SECURITY QUESTIONS**

**NOTES**

**WEBSITE**

**USERNAME**

**PASSWORD**

**SECURITY QUESTIONS**

**NOTES**

**WEBSITE**

**USERNAME**

**PASSWORD**

**SECURITY QUESTIONS**

**NOTES**

**WEBSITE**

**USERNAME**

**PASSWORD**

**SECURITY QUESTIONS**

**NOTES**

# WTF IS MY PASSWORD?

A

**WEBSITE**
_____

**USERNAME**
_____

**PASSWORD**
_____

**SECURITY QUESTIONS**
_____

**NOTES**

**WEBSITE**
_____

**USERNAME**
_____

**PASSWORD**
_____

**SECURITY QUESTIONS**
_____

**NOTES**

**WEBSITE**
_____

**USERNAME**
_____

**PASSWORD**
_____

**SECURITY QUESTIONS**
_____

**NOTES**

**WEBSITE**
_____

**USERNAME**
_____

**PASSWORD**
_____

**SECURITY QUESTIONS**
_____

**NOTES**

# WTF IS MY PASSWORD?

A

**WEBSITE**

_____

**USERNAME**

_____

**PASSWORD**

_____

**SECURITY QUESTIONS**

_____

**NOTES**

**WEBSITE**

_____

**USERNAME**

_____

**PASSWORD**

_____

**SECURITY QUESTIONS**

_____

**NOTES**

**WEBSITE**

_____

**USERNAME**

_____

**PASSWORD**

_____

**SECURITY QUESTIONS**

_____

**NOTES**

**WEBSITE**

_____

**USERNAME**

_____

**PASSWORD**

_____

**SECURITY QUESTIONS**

_____

**NOTES**

# WTF IS MY PASSWORD?

B

**WEBSITE**

**USERNAME**

**PASSWORD**

**SECURITY QUESTIONS**

NOTES

**WEBSITE**

**USERNAME**

**PASSWORD**

**SECURITY QUESTIONS**

NOTES

**WEBSITE**

**USERNAME**

**PASSWORD**

**SECURITY QUESTIONS**

NOTES

**WEBSITE**

**USERNAME**

**PASSWORD**

**SECURITY QUESTIONS**

NOTES

# WTF IS MY PASSWORD?

B

**WEBSITE**
_____

**USERNAME**
_____

**PASSWORD**
_____

**SECURITY QUESTIONS**
_____

**NOTES**

**WEBSITE**
_____

**USERNAME**
_____

**PASSWORD**
_____

**SECURITY QUESTIONS**
_____

**NOTES**

**WEBSITE**
_____

**USERNAME**
_____

**PASSWORD**
_____

**SECURITY QUESTIONS**
_____

**NOTES**

**WEBSITE**
_____

**USERNAME**
_____

**PASSWORD**
_____

**SECURITY QUESTIONS**
_____

**NOTES**

# WTF IS MY PASSWORD?

B

**WEBSITE**
_____

**USERNAME**
_____

**PASSWORD**
_____

**SECURITY QUESTIONS**
_____

**NOTES**

---

**WEBSITE**
_____

**USERNAME**
_____

**PASSWORD**
_____

**SECURITY QUESTIONS**
_____

**NOTES**

---

**WEBSITE**
_____

**USERNAME**
_____

**PASSWORD**
_____

**SECURITY QUESTIONS**
_____

**NOTES**

---

**WEBSITE**
_____

**USERNAME**
_____

**PASSWORD**
_____

**SECURITY QUESTIONS**
_____

**NOTES**

# WTF IS MY PASSWORD?

C

**WEBSITE**
_____

**USERNAME**
_____

**PASSWORD**
_____

**SECURITY QUESTIONS**
_____

**NOTES**

---

**WEBSITE**
_____

**USERNAME**
_____

**PASSWORD**
_____

**SECURITY QUESTIONS**
_____

**NOTES**

---

**WEBSITE**
_____

**USERNAME**
_____

**PASSWORD**
_____

**SECURITY QUESTIONS**
_____

**NOTES**

---

**WEBSITE**
_____

**USERNAME**
_____

**PASSWORD**
_____

**SECURITY QUESTIONS**
_____

**NOTES**

# WTF IS MY PASSWORD?

C

**WEBSITE**
_____

**USERNAME**
_____

**PASSWORD**
_____

**SECURITY QUESTIONS**
_____

**NOTES**

**WEBSITE**
_____

**USERNAME**
_____

**PASSWORD**
_____

**SECURITY QUESTIONS**
_____

**NOTES**

**WEBSITE**
_____

**USERNAME**
_____

**PASSWORD**
_____

**SECURITY QUESTIONS**
_____

**NOTES**

**WEBSITE**
_____

**USERNAME**
_____

**PASSWORD**
_____

**SECURITY QUESTIONS**
_____

**NOTES**

# WTF IS MY PASSWORD?

C

**WEBSITE**
_____
**USERNAME**
_____
**PASSWORD**
_____
**SECURITY QUESTIONS**
_____

NOTES

**WEBSITE**
_____
**USERNAME**
_____
**PASSWORD**
_____
**SECURITY QUESTIONS**
_____

NOTES

**WEBSITE**
_____
**USERNAME**
_____
**PASSWORD**
_____
**SECURITY QUESTIONS**
_____

NOTES

**WEBSITE**
_____
**USERNAME**
_____
**PASSWORD**
_____
**SECURITY QUESTIONS**
_____

NOTES

# WTF IS MY PASSWORD?

D

**WEBSITE**
_____
**USERNAME**
_____
**PASSWORD**
_____
**SECURITY QUESTIONS**
_____

**NOTES**

**WEBSITE**
_____
**USERNAME**
_____
**PASSWORD**
_____
**SECURITY QUESTIONS**
_____

**NOTES**

**WEBSITE**
_____
**USERNAME**
_____
**PASSWORD**
_____
**SECURITY QUESTIONS**
_____

**NOTES**

**WEBSITE**
_____
**USERNAME**
_____
**PASSWORD**
_____
**SECURITY QUESTIONS**
_____

**NOTES**

# WTF IS MY PASSWORD?

**D**

**WEBSITE**

**USERNAME**

**PASSWORD**

**SECURITY QUESTIONS**

**NOTES**

**WEBSITE**

**USERNAME**

**PASSWORD**

**SECURITY QUESTIONS**

**NOTES**

**WEBSITE**

**USERNAME**

**PASSWORD**

**SECURITY QUESTIONS**

**NOTES**

**WEBSITE**

**USERNAME**

**PASSWORD**

**SECURITY QUESTIONS**

**NOTES**

# WTF IS MY PASSWORD?

D

**WEBSITE**
_____

**USERNAME**
_____

**PASSWORD**
_____

**SECURITY QUESTIONS**
_____

**NOTES**

**WEBSITE**
_____

**USERNAME**
_____

**PASSWORD**
_____

**SECURITY QUESTIONS**
_____

**NOTES**

**WEBSITE**
_____

**USERNAME**
_____

**PASSWORD**
_____

**SECURITY QUESTIONS**
_____

**NOTES**

**WEBSITE**
_____

**USERNAME**
_____

**PASSWORD**
_____

**SECURITY QUESTIONS**
_____

**NOTES**

# WTF IS MY PASSWORD?

E

**WEBSITE**
_____

**USERNAME**
_____

**PASSWORD**
_____

**SECURITY QUESTIONS**
_____

**NOTES**

**WEBSITE**
_____

**USERNAME**
_____

**PASSWORD**
_____

**SECURITY QUESTIONS**
_____

**NOTES**

**WEBSITE**
_____

**USERNAME**
_____

**PASSWORD**
_____

**SECURITY QUESTIONS**
_____

**NOTES**

**WEBSITE**
_____

**USERNAME**
_____

**PASSWORD**
_____

**SECURITY QUESTIONS**
_____

**NOTES**

# WTF IS MY PASSWORD?

**WEBSITE**
_____

**USERNAME**
_____

**PASSWORD**
_____

**SECURITY QUESTIONS**
_____

**NOTES**

**WEBSITE**
_____

**USERNAME**
_____

**PASSWORD**
_____

**SECURITY QUESTIONS**
_____

**NOTES**

**WEBSITE**
_____

**USERNAME**
_____

**PASSWORD**
_____

**SECURITY QUESTIONS**
_____

**NOTES**

**WEBSITE**
_____

**USERNAME**
_____

**PASSWORD**
_____

**SECURITY QUESTIONS**
_____

**NOTES**

# WTF IS MY PASSWORD?

E

**WEBSITE**

---

**USERNAME**

---

**PASSWORD**

---

**SECURITY QUESTIONS**

---

**NOTES**

**WEBSITE**

---

**USERNAME**

---

**PASSWORD**

---

**SECURITY QUESTIONS**

---

**NOTES**

**WEBSITE**

---

**USERNAME**

---

**PASSWORD**

---

**SECURITY QUESTIONS**

---

**NOTES**

**WEBSITE**

---

**USERNAME**

---

**PASSWORD**

---

**SECURITY QUESTIONS**

---

**NOTES**

# WTF IS MY PASSWORD?

F

**WEBSITE**
_____
**USERNAME**
_____
**PASSWORD**
_____
**SECURITY QUESTIONS**
_____

**NOTES**

**WEBSITE**
_____
**USERNAME**
_____
**PASSWORD**
_____
**SECURITY QUESTIONS**
_____

**NOTES**

**WEBSITE**
_____
**USERNAME**
_____
**PASSWORD**
_____
**SECURITY QUESTIONS**
_____

**NOTES**

**WEBSITE**
_____
**USERNAME**
_____
**PASSWORD**
_____
**SECURITY QUESTIONS**
_____

**NOTES**

# WTF IS MY PASSWORD?

F

**WEBSITE**

_____

**USERNAME**

_____

**PASSWORD**

_____

**SECURITY QUESTIONS**

_____

**NOTES**

**WEBSITE**

_____

**USERNAME**

_____

**PASSWORD**

_____

**SECURITY QUESTIONS**

_____

**NOTES**

**WEBSITE**

_____

**USERNAME**

_____

**PASSWORD**

_____

**SECURITY QUESTIONS**

_____

**NOTES**

**WEBSITE**

_____

**USERNAME**

_____

**PASSWORD**

_____

**SECURITY QUESTIONS**

_____

**NOTES**

# WTF IS MY PASSWORD?

F

**WEBSITE**
_____

**USERNAME**
_____

**PASSWORD**
_____

**SECURITY QUESTIONS**
_____

**NOTES**

**WEBSITE**
_____

**USERNAME**
_____

**PASSWORD**
_____

**SECURITY QUESTIONS**
_____

**NOTES**

**WEBSITE**
_____

**USERNAME**
_____

**PASSWORD**
_____

**SECURITY QUESTIONS**
_____

**NOTES**

**WEBSITE**
_____

**USERNAME**
_____

**PASSWORD**
_____

**SECURITY QUESTIONS**
_____

**NOTES**

# WTF IS MY PASSWORD?

G

**WEBSITE**
_____
**USERNAME**
_____
**PASSWORD**
_____
**SECURITY QUESTIONS**
_____

**NOTES**

**WEBSITE**
_____
**USERNAME**
_____
**PASSWORD**
_____
**SECURITY QUESTIONS**
_____

**NOTES**

**WEBSITE**
_____
**USERNAME**
_____
**PASSWORD**
_____
**SECURITY QUESTIONS**
_____

**NOTES**

**WEBSITE**
_____
**USERNAME**
_____
**PASSWORD**
_____
**SECURITY QUESTIONS**
_____

**NOTES**

# WTF IS MY PASSWORD?

G

**WEBSITE**
_____

**USERNAME**
_____

**PASSWORD**
_____

**SECURITY QUESTIONS**
_____

**NOTES**

**WEBSITE**
_____

**USERNAME**
_____

**PASSWORD**
_____

**SECURITY QUESTIONS**
_____

**NOTES**

**WEBSITE**
_____

**USERNAME**
_____

**PASSWORD**
_____

**SECURITY QUESTIONS**
_____

**NOTES**

**WEBSITE**
_____

**USERNAME**
_____

**PASSWORD**
_____

**SECURITY QUESTIONS**
_____

**NOTES**

# WTF IS MY PASSWORD?

G

**WEBSITE**
_____
**USERNAME**
_____
**PASSWORD**
_____
**SECURITY QUESTIONS**
_____

**NOTES**

**WEBSITE**
_____
**USERNAME**
_____
**PASSWORD**
_____
**SECURITY QUESTIONS**
_____

**NOTES**

**WEBSITE**
_____
**USERNAME**
_____
**PASSWORD**
_____
**SECURITY QUESTIONS**
_____

**NOTES**

**WEBSITE**
_____
**USERNAME**
_____
**PASSWORD**
_____
**SECURITY QUESTIONS**
_____

**NOTES**

# WTF IS MY PASSWORD?

**WEBSITE**
_____
**USERNAME**
_____
**PASSWORD**
_____
**SECURITY QUESTIONS**
_____

**NOTES**

**WEBSITE**
_____
**USERNAME**
_____
**PASSWORD**
_____
**SECURITY QUESTIONS**
_____

**NOTES**

**WEBSITE**
_____
**USERNAME**
_____
**PASSWORD**
_____
**SECURITY QUESTIONS**
_____

**NOTES**

**WEBSITE**
_____
**USERNAME**
_____
**PASSWORD**
_____
**SECURITY QUESTIONS**
_____

**NOTES**

# WTF IS MY PASSWORD?

**WEBSITE**
_____

**USERNAME**
_____

**PASSWORD**
_____

**SECURITY QUESTIONS**
_____

**NOTES**

**WEBSITE**
_____

**USERNAME**
_____

**PASSWORD**
_____

**SECURITY QUESTIONS**
_____

**NOTES**

**WEBSITE**
_____

**USERNAME**
_____

**PASSWORD**
_____

**SECURITY QUESTIONS**
_____

**NOTES**

**WEBSITE**
_____

**USERNAME**
_____

**PASSWORD**
_____

**SECURITY QUESTIONS**
_____

**NOTES**

# WTF IS MY PASSWORD?

H

**WEBSITE**

_____

**USERNAME**

_____

**PASSWORD**

_____

**SECURITY QUESTIONS**

_____

**NOTES**

**WEBSITE**

_____

**USERNAME**

_____

**PASSWORD**

_____

**SECURITY QUESTIONS**

_____

**NOTES**

**WEBSITE**

_____

**USERNAME**

_____

**PASSWORD**

_____

**SECURITY QUESTIONS**

_____

**NOTES**

**WEBSITE**

_____

**USERNAME**

_____

**PASSWORD**

_____

**SECURITY QUESTIONS**

_____

**NOTES**

# WTF IS MY PASSWORD?

**WEBSITE**

_____

**USERNAME**

_____

**PASSWORD**

_____

**SECURITY QUESTIONS**

_____

**NOTES**

**WEBSITE**

_____

**USERNAME**

_____

**PASSWORD**

_____

**SECURITY QUESTIONS**

_____

**NOTES**

**WEBSITE**

_____

**USERNAME**

_____

**PASSWORD**

_____

**SECURITY QUESTIONS**

_____

**NOTES**

**WEBSITE**

_____

**USERNAME**

_____

**PASSWORD**

_____

**SECURITY QUESTIONS**

_____

**NOTES**

# WTF IS MY PASSWORD?

**WEBSITE**

**USERNAME**

**PASSWORD**

**SECURITY QUESTIONS**

**NOTES**

**WEBSITE**

**USERNAME**

**PASSWORD**

**SECURITY QUESTIONS**

**NOTES**

**WEBSITE**

**USERNAME**

**PASSWORD**

**SECURITY QUESTIONS**

**NOTES**

**WEBSITE**

**USERNAME**

**PASSWORD**

**SECURITY QUESTIONS**

**NOTES**

# WTF IS MY PASSWORD?

**WEBSITE**
_____
**USERNAME**
_____
**PASSWORD**
_____
**SECURITY QUESTIONS**
_____

**NOTES**

**WEBSITE**
_____
**USERNAME**
_____
**PASSWORD**
_____
**SECURITY QUESTIONS**
_____

**NOTES**

**WEBSITE**
_____
**USERNAME**
_____
**PASSWORD**
_____
**SECURITY QUESTIONS**
_____

**NOTES**

**WEBSITE**
_____
**USERNAME**
_____
**PASSWORD**
_____
**SECURITY QUESTIONS**
_____

**NOTES**

# WTF IS MY PASSWORD?

J

**WEBSITE**
_____

**USERNAME**
_____

**PASSWORD**
_____

**SECURITY QUESTIONS**
_____

**NOTES**

**WEBSITE**
_____

**USERNAME**
_____

**PASSWORD**
_____

**SECURITY QUESTIONS**
_____

**NOTES**

**WEBSITE**
_____

**USERNAME**
_____

**PASSWORD**
_____

**SECURITY QUESTIONS**
_____

**NOTES**

**WEBSITE**
_____

**USERNAME**
_____

**PASSWORD**
_____

**SECURITY QUESTIONS**
_____

**NOTES**

# WTF IS MY PASSWORD?

J

**WEBSITE**
_____
**USERNAME**
_____
**PASSWORD**
_____
**SECURITY QUESTIONS**
_____

**NOTES**

**WEBSITE**
_____
**USERNAME**
_____
**PASSWORD**
_____
**SECURITY QUESTIONS**
_____

**NOTES**

**WEBSITE**
_____
**USERNAME**
_____
**PASSWORD**
_____
**SECURITY QUESTIONS**
_____

**NOTES**

**WEBSITE**
_____
**USERNAME**
_____
**PASSWORD**
_____
**SECURITY QUESTIONS**
_____

**NOTES**

# WTF IS MY PASSWORD?

J

**WEBSITE**
_____

**USERNAME**
_____

**PASSWORD**
_____

**SECURITY QUESTIONS**
_____

**WEBSITE**
_____

**USERNAME**
_____

**PASSWORD**
_____

**SECURITY QUESTIONS**
_____

**NOTES**

**WEBSITE**
_____

**USERNAME**
_____

**PASSWORD**
_____

**SECURITY QUESTIONS**
_____

**NOTES**

**WEBSITE**
_____

**USERNAME**
_____

**PASSWORD**
_____

**SECURITY QUESTIONS**
_____

**NOTES**

# WTF IS MY PASSWORD?

K

**WEBSITE**

_____

**USERNAME**

_____

**PASSWORD**

_____

**SECURITY QUESTIONS**

_____

**NOTES**

**WEBSITE**

_____

**USERNAME**

_____

**PASSWORD**

_____

**SECURITY QUESTIONS**

_____

**NOTES**

**WEBSITE**

_____

**USERNAME**

_____

**PASSWORD**

_____

**SECURITY QUESTIONS**

_____

**NOTES**

**WEBSITE**

_____

**USERNAME**

_____

**PASSWORD**

_____

**SECURITY QUESTIONS**

_____

**NOTES**

# WTF IS MY PASSWORD?

K

**WEBSITE**
_____

**USERNAME**
_____

**PASSWORD**
_____

**SECURITY QUESTIONS**
_____

**NOTES**

**WEBSITE**
_____

**USERNAME**
_____

**PASSWORD**
_____

**SECURITY QUESTIONS**
_____

**NOTES**

**WEBSITE**
_____

**USERNAME**
_____

**PASSWORD**
_____

**SECURITY QUESTIONS**
_____

**NOTES**

**WEBSITE**
_____

**USERNAME**
_____

**PASSWORD**
_____

**SECURITY QUESTIONS**
_____

**NOTES**

# WTF IS MY PASSWORD?

K

**WEBSITE**
_____
**USERNAME**
_____
**PASSWORD**
_____
**SECURITY QUESTIONS**
_____

**NOTES**

**WEBSITE**
_____
**USERNAME**
_____
**PASSWORD**
_____
**SECURITY QUESTIONS**
_____

**NOTES**

**WEBSITE**
_____
**USERNAME**
_____
**PASSWORD**
_____
**SECURITY QUESTIONS**
_____

**NOTES**

**WEBSITE**
_____
**USERNAME**
_____
**PASSWORD**
_____
**SECURITY QUESTIONS**
_____

**NOTES**

# WTF IS MY PASSWORD?

L

**WEBSITE**

**USERNAME**

**PASSWORD**

**SECURITY QUESTIONS**

**NOTES**

**WEBSITE**

**USERNAME**

**PASSWORD**

**SECURITY QUESTIONS**

**NOTES**

**WEBSITE**

**USERNAME**

**PASSWORD**

**SECURITY QUESTIONS**

**NOTES**

**WEBSITE**

**USERNAME**

**PASSWORD**

**SECURITY QUESTIONS**

**NOTES**

# WTF IS MY PASSWORD?

L

**WEBSITE**
_____

**USERNAME**
_____

**PASSWORD**
_____

**SECURITY QUESTIONS**
_____

**NOTES**

**WEBSITE**
_____

**USERNAME**
_____

**PASSWORD**
_____

**SECURITY QUESTIONS**
_____

**NOTES**

**WEBSITE**
_____

**USERNAME**
_____

**PASSWORD**
_____

**SECURITY QUESTIONS**
_____

**NOTES**

**WEBSITE**
_____

**USERNAME**
_____

**PASSWORD**
_____

**SECURITY QUESTIONS**
_____

**NOTES**

# WTF IS MY PASSWORD?

L

**WEBSITE**
_____

**USERNAME**
_____

**PASSWORD**
_____

**SECURITY QUESTIONS**
_____

**NOTES**

**WEBSITE**
_____

**USERNAME**
_____

**PASSWORD**
_____

**SECURITY QUESTIONS**
_____

**NOTES**

**WEBSITE**
_____

**USERNAME**
_____

**PASSWORD**
_____

**SECURITY QUESTIONS**
_____

**NOTES**

**WEBSITE**
_____

**USERNAME**
_____

**PASSWORD**
_____

**SECURITY QUESTIONS**
_____

**NOTES**

# WTF IS MY PASSWORD?

**WEBSITE**

_____

**USERNAME**

_____

**PASSWORD**

_____

**SECURITY QUESTIONS**

_____

**NOTES**

**WEBSITE**

_____

**USERNAME**

_____

**PASSWORD**

_____

**SECURITY QUESTIONS**

_____

**NOTES**

**WEBSITE**

_____

**USERNAME**

_____

**PASSWORD**

_____

**SECURITY QUESTIONS**

_____

**NOTES**

**WEBSITE**

_____

**USERNAME**

_____

**PASSWORD**

_____

**SECURITY QUESTIONS**

_____

**NOTES**

# WTF IS MY PASSWORD?

M

**WEBSITE**
_____
**USERNAME**
_____
**PASSWORD**
_____
**SECURITY QUESTIONS**
_____

**NOTES**

**WEBSITE**
_____
**USERNAME**
_____
**PASSWORD**
_____
**SECURITY QUESTIONS**
_____

**NOTES**

**WEBSITE**
_____
**USERNAME**
_____
**PASSWORD**
_____
**SECURITY QUESTIONS**
_____

**NOTES**

**WEBSITE**
_____
**USERNAME**
_____
**PASSWORD**
_____
**SECURITY QUESTIONS**
_____

**NOTES**

# WTF IS MY PASSWORD?

M

**WEBSITE**

**USERNAME**

**PASSWORD**

**SECURITY QUESTIONS**

**WEBSITE**

**USERNAME**

**PASSWORD**

**SECURITY QUESTIONS**

**WEBSITE**

**USERNAME**

**PASSWORD**

**SECURITY QUESTIONS**

**WEBSITE**

**USERNAME**

**PASSWORD**

**SECURITY QUESTIONS**

# WTF IS MY PASSWORD?

**WEBSITE**

**USERNAME**

**PASSWORD**

**SECURITY QUESTIONS**

**NOTES**

**WEBSITE**

**USERNAME**

**PASSWORD**

**SECURITY QUESTIONS**

**NOTES**

**WEBSITE**

**USERNAME**

**PASSWORD**

**SECURITY QUESTIONS**

**NOTES**

**WEBSITE**

**USERNAME**

**PASSWORD**

**SECURITY QUESTIONS**

**NOTES**

# WTF IS MY PASSWORD?

N

**WEBSITE**
_____

**USERNAME**
_____

**PASSWORD**
_____

**SECURITY QUESTIONS**
_____

NOTES

**WEBSITE**
_____

**USERNAME**
_____

**PASSWORD**
_____

**SECURITY QUESTIONS**
_____

NOTES

**WEBSITE**
_____

**USERNAME**
_____

**PASSWORD**
_____

**SECURITY QUESTIONS**
_____

NOTES

**WEBSITE**
_____

**USERNAME**
_____

**PASSWORD**
_____

**SECURITY QUESTIONS**
_____

NOTES

# WTF IS MY PASSWORD?

N

**WEBSITE**

_____

**USERNAME**

_____

**PASSWORD**

_____

**SECURITY QUESTIONS**

_____

**NOTES**

**WEBSITE**

_____

**USERNAME**

_____

**PASSWORD**

_____

**SECURITY QUESTIONS**

_____

**NOTES**

**WEBSITE**

_____

**USERNAME**

_____

**PASSWORD**

_____

**SECURITY QUESTIONS**

_____

**NOTES**

**WEBSITE**

_____

**USERNAME**

_____

**PASSWORD**

_____

**SECURITY QUESTIONS**

_____

**NOTES**

# WTF IS MY PASSWORD?

**WEBSITE**
_____
**USERNAME**
_____
**PASSWORD**
_____
**SECURITY QUESTIONS**
_____

**NOTES**

**WEBSITE**
_____
**USERNAME**
_____
**PASSWORD**
_____
**SECURITY QUESTIONS**
_____

**NOTES**

**WEBSITE**
_____
**USERNAME**
_____
**PASSWORD**
_____
**SECURITY QUESTIONS**
_____

**NOTES**

**WEBSITE**
_____
**USERNAME**
_____
**PASSWORD**
_____
**SECURITY QUESTIONS**
_____

**NOTES**

# WTF IS MY PASSWORD?

O

**WEBSITE**
_____
**USERNAME**
_____
**PASSWORD**
_____
**SECURITY QUESTIONS**
_____

NOTES

**WEBSITE**
_____
**USERNAME**
_____
**PASSWORD**
_____
**SECURITY QUESTIONS**
_____

NOTES

**WEBSITE**
_____
**USERNAME**
_____
**PASSWORD**
_____
**SECURITY QUESTIONS**
_____

NOTES

**WEBSITE**
_____
**USERNAME**
_____
**PASSWORD**
_____
**SECURITY QUESTIONS**
_____

NOTES

# WTF IS MY PASSWORD?

**WEBSITE**
_____
**USERNAME**
_____
**PASSWORD**
_____
**SECURITY QUESTIONS**
_____

**NOTES**

**WEBSITE**
_____
**USERNAME**
_____
**PASSWORD**
_____
**SECURITY QUESTIONS**
_____

**NOTES**

**WEBSITE**
_____
**USERNAME**
_____
**PASSWORD**
_____
**SECURITY QUESTIONS**
_____

**NOTES**

**WEBSITE**
_____
**USERNAME**
_____
**PASSWORD**
_____
**SECURITY QUESTIONS**
_____

**NOTES**

# WTF IS MY PASSWORD?

P

**WEBSITE**
_____
**USERNAME**
_____
**PASSWORD**
_____
**SECURITY QUESTIONS**
_____

**NOTES**

**WEBSITE**
_____
**USERNAME**
_____
**PASSWORD**
_____
**SECURITY QUESTIONS**
_____

**NOTES**

**WEBSITE**
_____
**USERNAME**
_____
**PASSWORD**
_____
**SECURITY QUESTIONS**
_____

**NOTES**

**WEBSITE**
_____
**USERNAME**
_____
**PASSWORD**
_____
**SECURITY QUESTIONS**
_____

**NOTES**

# WTF IS MY PASSWORD?

P

**WEBSITE**

_____

**USERNAME**

_____

**PASSWORD**

_____

**SECURITY QUESTIONS**

_____

**NOTES**

**WEBSITE**

_____

**USERNAME**

_____

**PASSWORD**

_____

**SECURITY QUESTIONS**

_____

**NOTES**

**WEBSITE**

_____

**USERNAME**

_____

**PASSWORD**

_____

**SECURITY QUESTIONS**

_____

**NOTES**

**WEBSITE**

_____

**USERNAME**

_____

**PASSWORD**

_____

**SECURITY QUESTIONS**

_____

**NOTES**

# WTF IS MY PASSWORD?

P

**WEBSITE**

**USERNAME**

**PASSWORD**

**SECURITY QUESTIONS**

**NOTES**

**WEBSITE**

**USERNAME**

**PASSWORD**

**SECURITY QUESTIONS**

**NOTES**

**WEBSITE**

**USERNAME**

**PASSWORD**

**SECURITY QUESTIONS**

**NOTES**

**WEBSITE**

**USERNAME**

**PASSWORD**

**SECURITY QUESTIONS**

**NOTES**

# WTF IS MY PASSWORD?

Q

**WEBSITE**
_____
**USERNAME**
_____
**PASSWORD**
_____
**SECURITY QUESTIONS**
_____

**NOTES**

**WEBSITE**
_____
**USERNAME**
_____
**PASSWORD**
_____
**SECURITY QUESTIONS**
_____

**NOTES**

**WEBSITE**
_____
**USERNAME**
_____
**PASSWORD**
_____
**SECURITY QUESTIONS**
_____

**NOTES**

**WEBSITE**
_____
**USERNAME**
_____
**PASSWORD**
_____
**SECURITY QUESTIONS**
_____

**NOTES**

# WTF IS MY PASSWORD?

**Q**

**WEBSITE**

_____

**USERNAME**

_____

**PASSWORD**

_____

**SECURITY QUESTIONS**

_____

**NOTES**

**WEBSITE**

_____

**USERNAME**

_____

**PASSWORD**

_____

**SECURITY QUESTIONS**

_____

**NOTES**

**WEBSITE**

_____

**USERNAME**

_____

**PASSWORD**

_____

**SECURITY QUESTIONS**

_____

**NOTES**

**WEBSITE**

_____

**USERNAME**

_____

**PASSWORD**

_____

**SECURITY QUESTIONS**

_____

**NOTES**

# WTF IS MY PASSWORD?

Q

**WEBSITE**

_____

**USERNAME**

_____

**PASSWORD**

_____

**SECURITY QUESTIONS**

_____

**NOTES**

**WEBSITE**

_____

**USERNAME**

_____

**PASSWORD**

_____

**SECURITY QUESTIONS**

_____

**NOTES**

**WEBSITE**

_____

**USERNAME**

_____

**PASSWORD**

_____

**SECURITY QUESTIONS**

_____

**NOTES**

**WEBSITE**

_____

**USERNAME**

_____

**PASSWORD**

_____

**SECURITY QUESTIONS**

_____

**NOTES**

# WTF IS MY PASSWORD?

R

**WEBSITE**
_____
**USERNAME**
_____
**PASSWORD**
_____
**SECURITY QUESTIONS**
_____

**NOTES**

**WEBSITE**
_____
**USERNAME**
_____
**PASSWORD**
_____
**SECURITY QUESTIONS**
_____

**NOTES**

**WEBSITE**
_____
**USERNAME**
_____
**PASSWORD**
_____
**SECURITY QUESTIONS**
_____

**NOTES**

**WEBSITE**
_____
**USERNAME**
_____
**PASSWORD**
_____
**SECURITY QUESTIONS**
_____

**NOTES**

# WTF IS MY PASSWORD?

R

**WEBSITE**

_____

**USERNAME**

_____

**PASSWORD**

_____

**SECURITY QUESTIONS**

_____

**NOTES**

**WEBSITE**

_____

**USERNAME**

_____

**PASSWORD**

_____

**SECURITY QUESTIONS**

_____

**NOTES**

**WEBSITE**

_____

**USERNAME**

_____

**PASSWORD**

_____

**SECURITY QUESTIONS**

_____

**NOTES**

**WEBSITE**

_____

**USERNAME**

_____

**PASSWORD**

_____

**SECURITY QUESTIONS**

_____

**NOTES**

# WTF IS MY PASSWORD?

R

**NOTES**

**WEBSITE**
_____
**USERNAME**
_____
**PASSWORD**
_____
**SECURITY QUESTIONS**
_____

**NOTES**

**WEBSITE**
_____
**USERNAME**
_____
**PASSWORD**
_____
**SECURITY QUESTIONS**
_____

**NOTES**

**WEBSITE**
_____
**USERNAME**
_____
**PASSWORD**
_____
**SECURITY QUESTIONS**
_____

**NOTES**

**WEBSITE**
_____
**USERNAME**
_____
**PASSWORD**
_____
**SECURITY QUESTIONS**
_____

# WTF IS MY PASSWORD?

S

**WEBSITE**
_____

**USERNAME**
_____

**PASSWORD**
_____

**SECURITY QUESTIONS**
_____

**NOTES**

**WEBSITE**
_____

**USERNAME**
_____

**PASSWORD**
_____

**SECURITY QUESTIONS**
_____

**NOTES**

**WEBSITE**
_____

**USERNAME**
_____

**PASSWORD**
_____

**SECURITY QUESTIONS**
_____

**NOTES**

**WEBSITE**
_____

**USERNAME**
_____

**PASSWORD**
_____

**SECURITY QUESTIONS**
_____

**NOTES**

# WTF IS MY PASSWORD?

S

**WEBSITE**
_____

**USERNAME**
_____

**PASSWORD**
_____

**SECURITY QUESTIONS**
_____

**NOTES**

**WEBSITE**
_____

**USERNAME**
_____

**PASSWORD**
_____

**SECURITY QUESTIONS**
_____

**NOTES**

**WEBSITE**
_____

**USERNAME**
_____

**PASSWORD**
_____

**SECURITY QUESTIONS**
_____

**NOTES**

**WEBSITE**
_____

**USERNAME**
_____

**PASSWORD**
_____

**SECURITY QUESTIONS**
_____

**NOTES**

# WTF IS MY PASSWORD?

S

**NOTES**

**WEBSITE**

**USERNAME**

**PASSWORD**

**SECURITY QUESTIONS**

**NOTES**

**WEBSITE**

**USERNAME**

**PASSWORD**

**SECURITY QUESTIONS**

**NOTES**

**WEBSITE**

**USERNAME**

**PASSWORD**

**SECURITY QUESTIONS**

**NOTES**

**WEBSITE**

**USERNAME**

**PASSWORD**

**SECURITY QUESTIONS**

# WTF IS MY PASSWORD?

T

**WEBSITE**
_____
**USERNAME**
_____
**PASSWORD**
_____
**SECURITY QUESTIONS**
_____

**NOTES**

**WEBSITE**
_____
**USERNAME**
_____
**PASSWORD**
_____
**SECURITY QUESTIONS**
_____

**NOTES**

**WEBSITE**
_____
**USERNAME**
_____
**PASSWORD**
_____
**SECURITY QUESTIONS**
_____

**NOTES**

**WEBSITE**
_____
**USERNAME**
_____
**PASSWORD**
_____
**SECURITY QUESTIONS**
_____

**NOTES**

# WTF IS MY PASSWORD?

T

**WEBSITE**
_____

**USERNAME**
_____

**PASSWORD**
_____

**SECURITY QUESTIONS**
_____

**NOTES**

**WEBSITE**
_____

**USERNAME**
_____

**PASSWORD**
_____

**SECURITY QUESTIONS**
_____

**NOTES**

**WEBSITE**
_____

**USERNAME**
_____

**PASSWORD**
_____

**SECURITY QUESTIONS**
_____

**NOTES**

**WEBSITE**
_____

**USERNAME**
_____

**PASSWORD**
_____

**SECURITY QUESTIONS**
_____

**NOTES**

# WTF IS MY PASSWORD?

T

**WEBSITE**
_____
**USERNAME**
_____
**PASSWORD**
_____
**SECURITY QUESTIONS**
_____

**NOTES**

**WEBSITE**
_____
**USERNAME**
_____
**PASSWORD**
_____
**SECURITY QUESTIONS**
_____

**NOTES**

**WEBSITE**
_____
**USERNAME**
_____
**PASSWORD**
_____
**SECURITY QUESTIONS**
_____

**NOTES**

**WEBSITE**
_____
**USERNAME**
_____
**PASSWORD**
_____
**SECURITY QUESTIONS**
_____

**NOTES**

# WTF IS MY PASSWORD?

U

### WEBSITE
_____
### USERNAME
_____
### PASSWORD
_____
### SECURITY QUESTIONS
_____

**NOTES**

### WEBSITE
_____
### USERNAME
_____
### PASSWORD
_____
### SECURITY QUESTIONS
_____

**NOTES**

### WEBSITE
_____
### USERNAME
_____
### PASSWORD
_____
### SECURITY QUESTIONS
_____

**NOTES**

### WEBSITE
_____
### USERNAME
_____
### PASSWORD
_____
### SECURITY QUESTIONS
_____

**NOTES**

# WTF IS MY PASSWORD?

U

**WEBSITE**

_____

**USERNAME**

_____

**PASSWORD**

_____

**SECURITY QUESTIONS**

_____

**WEBSITE**

_____

**USERNAME**

_____

**PASSWORD**

_____

**SECURITY QUESTIONS**

_____

**WEBSITE**

_____

**USERNAME**

_____

**PASSWORD**

_____

**SECURITY QUESTIONS**

_____

**WEBSITE**

_____

**USERNAME**

_____

**PASSWORD**

_____

**SECURITY QUESTIONS**

_____

# WTF IS MY PASSWORD?

U

**WEBSITE**
_____

**USERNAME**
_____

**PASSWORD**
_____

**SECURITY QUESTIONS**
_____

**NOTES**

**WEBSITE**
_____

**USERNAME**
_____

**PASSWORD**
_____

**SECURITY QUESTIONS**
_____

**NOTES**

**WEBSITE**
_____

**USERNAME**
_____

**PASSWORD**
_____

**SECURITY QUESTIONS**
_____

**NOTES**

**WEBSITE**
_____

**USERNAME**
_____

**PASSWORD**
_____

**SECURITY QUESTIONS**
_____

**NOTES**

# WTF IS MY PASSWORD?

**WEBSITE**
_____
**USERNAME**
_____
**PASSWORD**
_____
**SECURITY QUESTIONS**
_____

**NOTES**

**WEBSITE**
_____
**USERNAME**
_____
**PASSWORD**
_____
**SECURITY QUESTIONS**
_____

**NOTES**

**WEBSITE**
_____
**USERNAME**
_____
**PASSWORD**
_____
**SECURITY QUESTIONS**
_____

**NOTES**

**WEBSITE**
_____
**USERNAME**
_____
**PASSWORD**
_____
**SECURITY QUESTIONS**
_____

**NOTES**

# WTF IS MY PASSWORD?

**WEBSITE**
_____

**USERNAME**
_____

**PASSWORD**
_____

**SECURITY QUESTIONS**
_____

**NOTES**

**WEBSITE**
_____

**USERNAME**
_____

**PASSWORD**
_____

**SECURITY QUESTIONS**
_____

**NOTES**

**WEBSITE**
_____

**USERNAME**
_____

**PASSWORD**
_____

**SECURITY QUESTIONS**
_____

**NOTES**

**WEBSITE**
_____

**USERNAME**
_____

**PASSWORD**
_____

**SECURITY QUESTIONS**
_____

**NOTES**

# WTF IS MY PASSWORD?

**WEBSITE**
_____

**USERNAME**
_____

**PASSWORD**
_____

**SECURITY QUESTIONS**
_____

**NOTES**

**WEBSITE**
_____

**USERNAME**
_____

**PASSWORD**
_____

**SECURITY QUESTIONS**
_____

**NOTES**

**WEBSITE**
_____

**USERNAME**
_____

**PASSWORD**
_____

**SECURITY QUESTIONS**
_____

**NOTES**

**WEBSITE**
_____

**USERNAME**
_____

**PASSWORD**
_____

**SECURITY QUESTIONS**
_____

**NOTES**

# WTF IS MY PASSWORD?

**WEBSITE**

_____

**USERNAME**

_____

**PASSWORD**

_____

**SECURITY QUESTIONS**

_____

**NOTES**

**WEBSITE**

_____

**USERNAME**

_____

**PASSWORD**

_____

**SECURITY QUESTIONS**

_____

**NOTES**

**WEBSITE**

_____

**USERNAME**

_____

**PASSWORD**

_____

**SECURITY QUESTIONS**

_____

**NOTES**

**WEBSITE**

_____

**USERNAME**

_____

**PASSWORD**

_____

**SECURITY QUESTIONS**

_____

**NOTES**

# WTF IS MY PASSWORD?

**WEBSITE**
_____

**USERNAME**
_____

**PASSWORD**
_____

**SECURITY QUESTIONS**
_____

**NOTES**

**WEBSITE**
_____

**USERNAME**
_____

**PASSWORD**
_____

**SECURITY QUESTIONS**
_____

**NOTES**

**WEBSITE**
_____

**USERNAME**
_____

**PASSWORD**
_____

**SECURITY QUESTIONS**
_____

**NOTES**

**WEBSITE**
_____

**USERNAME**
_____

**PASSWORD**
_____

**SECURITY QUESTIONS**
_____

**NOTES**

# WTF IS MY PASSWORD?

**WEBSITE**

_____

**USERNAME**

_____

**PASSWORD**

_____

**SECURITY QUESTIONS**

_____

**NOTES**

---

**WEBSITE**

_____

**USERNAME**

_____

**PASSWORD**

_____

**SECURITY QUESTIONS**

_____

**NOTES**

---

**WEBSITE**

_____

**USERNAME**

_____

**PASSWORD**

_____

**SECURITY QUESTIONS**

_____

**NOTES**

---

**WEBSITE**

_____

**USERNAME**

_____

**PASSWORD**

_____

**SECURITY QUESTIONS**

_____

**NOTES**

# WTF IS MY PASSWORD?

X

**WEBSITE**
_____

**USERNAME**
_____

**PASSWORD**
_____

**SECURITY QUESTIONS**
_____

**NOTES**

**WEBSITE**
_____

**USERNAME**
_____

**PASSWORD**
_____

**SECURITY QUESTIONS**
_____

**NOTES**

**WEBSITE**
_____

**USERNAME**
_____

**PASSWORD**
_____

**SECURITY QUESTIONS**
_____

**NOTES**

**WEBSITE**
_____

**USERNAME**
_____

**PASSWORD**
_____

**SECURITY QUESTIONS**
_____

**NOTES**

# WTF IS MY PASSWORD?

**WEBSITE**
_____
**USERNAME**
_____
**PASSWORD**
_____
**SECURITY QUESTIONS**
_____

**NOTES**

**WEBSITE**
_____
**USERNAME**
_____
**PASSWORD**
_____
**SECURITY QUESTIONS**
_____

**NOTES**

**WEBSITE**
_____
**USERNAME**
_____
**PASSWORD**
_____
**SECURITY QUESTIONS**
_____

**NOTES**

**WEBSITE**
_____
**USERNAME**
_____
**PASSWORD**
_____
**SECURITY QUESTIONS**
_____

**NOTES**

# WTF IS MY PASSWORD?

**WEBSITE**
_____

**USERNAME**
_____

**PASSWORD**
_____

**SECURITY QUESTIONS**
_____

**NOTES**

**WEBSITE**
_____

**USERNAME**
_____

**PASSWORD**
_____

**SECURITY QUESTIONS**
_____

**NOTES**

**WEBSITE**
_____

**USERNAME**
_____

**PASSWORD**
_____

**SECURITY QUESTIONS**
_____

**NOTES**

**WEBSITE**
_____

**USERNAME**
_____

**PASSWORD**
_____

**SECURITY QUESTIONS**
_____

**NOTES**

# WTF IS MY PASSWORD?

**WEBSITE**

_____

**USERNAME**

_____

**PASSWORD**

_____

**SECURITY QUESTIONS**

_____

**NOTES**

**WEBSITE**

_____

**USERNAME**

_____

**PASSWORD**

_____

**SECURITY QUESTIONS**

_____

**NOTES**

**WEBSITE**

_____

**USERNAME**

_____

**PASSWORD**

_____

**SECURITY QUESTIONS**

_____

**NOTES**

**WEBSITE**

_____

**USERNAME**

_____

**PASSWORD**

_____

**SECURITY QUESTIONS**

_____

**NOTES**

# WTF IS MY PASSWORD?

Y

**WEBSITE**
_____
**USERNAME**
_____
**PASSWORD**
_____
**SECURITY QUESTIONS**
_____

**NOTES**

**WEBSITE**
_____
**USERNAME**
_____
**PASSWORD**
_____
**SECURITY QUESTIONS**
_____

**NOTES**

**WEBSITE**
_____
**USERNAME**
_____
**PASSWORD**
_____
**SECURITY QUESTIONS**
_____

**NOTES**

**WEBSITE**
_____
**USERNAME**
_____
**PASSWORD**
_____
**SECURITY QUESTIONS**
_____

**NOTES**

# WTF IS MY PASSWORD?

Y

**NOTES**

**WEBSITE**
_____
**USERNAME**
_____
**PASSWORD**
_____
**SECURITY QUESTIONS**
_____

**NOTES**

**WEBSITE**
_____
**USERNAME**
_____
**PASSWORD**
_____
**SECURITY QUESTIONS**
_____

**NOTES**

**WEBSITE**
_____
**USERNAME**
_____
**PASSWORD**
_____
**SECURITY QUESTIONS**
_____

**NOTES**

**WEBSITE**
_____
**USERNAME**
_____
**PASSWORD**
_____
**SECURITY QUESTIONS**
_____

# WTF IS MY PASSWORD?

Z

**WEBSITE**
_____

**USERNAME**
_____

**PASSWORD**
_____

**SECURITY QUESTIONS**
_____

**NOTES**

**WEBSITE**
_____

**USERNAME**
_____

**PASSWORD**
_____

**SECURITY QUESTIONS**
_____

**NOTES**

**WEBSITE**
_____

**USERNAME**
_____

**PASSWORD**
_____

**SECURITY QUESTIONS**
_____

**NOTES**

**WEBSITE**
_____

**USERNAME**
_____

**PASSWORD**
_____

**SECURITY QUESTIONS**
_____

**NOTES**

# WTF IS MY PASSWORD?

**Z**

**NOTES**

WEBSITE

_____

USERNAME

_____

PASSWORD

_____

SECURITY QUESTIONS

_____

**NOTES**

WEBSITE

_____

USERNAME

_____

PASSWORD

_____

SECURITY QUESTIONS

_____

**NOTES**

WEBSITE

_____

USERNAME

_____

PASSWORD

_____

SECURITY QUESTIONS

_____

**NOTES**

WEBSITE

_____

USERNAME

_____

PASSWORD

_____

SECURITY QUESTIONS

_____

# WTF IS MY PASSWORD?

Z

**WEBSITE**
_____
**USERNAME**
_____
**PASSWORD**
_____
**SECURITY QUESTIONS**
_____

**NOTES**

**WEBSITE**
_____
**USERNAME**
_____
**PASSWORD**
_____
**SECURITY QUESTIONS**
_____

**NOTES**

**WEBSITE**
_____
**USERNAME**
_____
**PASSWORD**
_____
**SECURITY QUESTIONS**
_____

**NOTES**

**WEBSITE**
_____
**USERNAME**
_____
**PASSWORD**
_____
**SECURITY QUESTIONS**
_____

**NOTES**

## Just Write
## The Damn Thing!

_____
_____
_____
_____
_____
_____
_____
_____
_____
_____
_____
_____
_____
_____
_____
_____
_____
_____
_____
_____

*Just Write*
*The Damn Thing!*

_____

_____

_____

_____

_____

_____

_____

_____

_____

_____

_____

_____

_____

_____

_____

_____

_____

_____

*Just Write*
*The Damn Thing!*

_____

_____

_____

_____

_____

_____

_____

_____

_____

_____

_____

_____

_____

_____

_____

_____

_____

_____

_____

*Just Write The Damn Thing!*

_____
_____
_____
_____
_____
_____
_____
_____
_____
_____
_____
_____
_____
_____
_____
_____
_____
_____
_____
_____

*Just Write The Damn Thing!*

_____

_____

_____

_____

_____

_____

_____

_____

_____

_____

_____

_____

_____

_____

_____

_____

_____

_____

*Just Write
The Damn Thing!*

# Thank you!

We hope you enjoyed our book.

As a small family company, your feedback is very important to us .

Please let us know how you like our book at :

**pickme.readme@gmail.com**